MW00669169

UNDERSTANDING ANNABERG

A Brief History of Estate Annaberg on St. John, U. S. Virgin Islands

With A Closer Look at the Annaberg Factory Complex
and How Sugar Was Made

Researched, Written, and Compiled
by David W. Knight
Director of Danish West Indies Research
Virgin Islands Historical & Genealogical Resource Center

Research for this work was funded through a cooperative
agreement between the Georgia Trust for Historic Preservation
and
the National Park Service

First printing 2002   ISBN: 1-891610-08-2

Cover photograph: Carl and Amy Francis pose with their son Earl in front of
their home in "Francis' Castle" (the Annaberg windmill tower) circa 1916
(Royal Library Photograph Collection, Copenhagen, Denmark)

This work would not have been possible without
the able assistance of the following individuals:

Laurette de Tousard Prime, Archival Research Associate and Editor
George F. Tyson, Danish West Indies Resource Consultant
Paul E. Olsen, Chief Consultant Danish National Archives
Palle Sigaard, Danish West Indies Archive Consultant
Gary T. Horlacher, Danish, Norwegian, and German Translator
Gabrielle La Place, French Translator
Lief C. Larsen, Danish Translator and Resource Consultant
Douglas V. Armstrong, Archaeological Consultant
Henry B. Hoff, Genealogical Consultant
Per Nielsen, Danish West Indies Genealogical Consultant
Karen Munk-Nielsen, Danish Archives Research Assistant
Terry & Chuck Pishko, Reviewers and Field Survey Assistants
Jessica Bishop & David Knight Jr., Field Survey Assistants

Special thanks to:
Bob Blythe of the National Park Service Southeast Regional Office in
Atlanta for his patient review and knowledgeable guidance,
and Rafe Boulon, Ken Wild, and Lori Lee
of the Virgin Islands National Park on St. John for their support and
encouragement throughout the project.

Contents

(Photograph by B. Biziewski, 2001 [courtesy the St. John Historical Society])

Foreword

Today, the ruins of the once grand Annaberg sugar factory stand in bold testament to a time when sugar was king. But to fully grasp the broader importance of this site, it is necessary to look beyond the finely cut coral keystones and carefully laid ballast brick, and explore the complex tapestry of lives and events that mark this spot as a eloquent monument to our common human heritage. For amidst these crumbling walls echo a multitude of voices, and each has its own tale to tell. For some, the story begins in the sweltering jungles of West Africa; for others, on a cold and rocky Northern European coast; for still others, it begins on these very shores. Some sought wealth and opportunity; others, escape from strife or ethnic persecution. The majority, found only enslavement and misery; few, very few, endured.

1

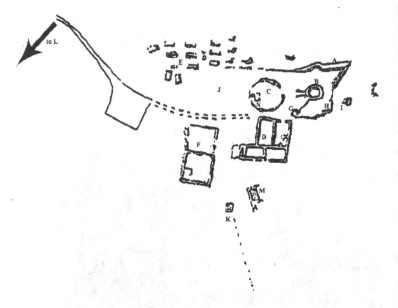

Site Map of the Annaberg Factory Complex

The ruins of the Annaberg factory complex stand out as a prominent landmark amidst the rapidly diminishing cultural landscape of St. John's North Shore. A sturdy retaining wall [A], constructed along the north, east, and southeast sides of a knoll, supports an irregular level platform that provides the setting for the site's masonry windmill tower [B] and animal mill [C]. The walls of the animal mill rotunda serve to retain the platform to the northwest, west, and southwest. The ruins of the site's primary processing facility (factory building) [D] stand downslope from the mill platform, roughly 48 feet south of the center point of the animal mill. Fragments of at least twenty-one laborers' houses [E] with rubble masonry foundations can be discerned on the northeast, north, and northwest slopes of the knoll below the retaining walls. Additionally, excavated flat areas on the hillside denote where other dwellings of less substantial construction once stood. In addition to these elements, the Annaberg factory complex also comprises the ruined remains of a mule pen [F], bake oven [G], a sick house with a cistern and detention cell [H], a privy [I], magass house [J], two elevated cisterns with a connecting aqueduct [K], a well with a drinking trough [L], and an unidentified structure [M]. An early twentieth century cook house has also been preserved on the site [N].

2

Historical Background

On March 25, 1718, the governor of the Danish West Indies and Guinea Company colony of St. Thomas, Eric Bredal, accompanied by five soldiers, twenty planters, and sixteen enslaved laborers, landed in Coral Bay to claim the island of St. John in the name of the Danish Crown. After selecting a site for the Company plantation, the governor instructed the planters to indicate the parcels of land they intended to occupy. Their mission accomplished, Bradel and his party beat a hasty retreat back to St. Thomas, where they awaited any repercussions that may have been prompted by their actions. Once it became evident that the Danish claim and occupation of St. John would not be vigorously opposed by the British, who for some time had maintained legitimate possession of the island, the planters moved quickly to establish their new holdings [Larsen, 1986; Bro-Jørgensen, 1966].

Since few documents remain from the era, little is known of the early years of plantation development on St. John. From the earliest existing tax records, compiled in the year 1728, we can deduce that the first nine officially sanctioned private land holdings were taken up in the years 1718 and 1719 along St. John's northwest coast, between what are today known as estates *Caneel Bay* and *Cinnamon Bay* [LD, 1722; SJLL, 1728]. From a letter of report sent by Governor Bredal to the Danish West Indies and Guinea Company home office in Copenhagen, we learn that Peter Durloo, a Dutchman who had left Curaçâo to take up residency on St. Thomas near the close of the seventeenth century, was the first of the Danish-sponsored settlers to occupy a parcel of land on St. John, "...as none else dared because of the threat from other nations" [LD, 1720-22].

As cautious as the initial Danish-backed settlers of St. John may have been, it was not long before Durloo was joined by an increasing number of willing colonists. Among these earliest settlers were a small group of Huguenot refugees from the French islands of the Caribbean. With the revocation of the Edict of Nantes in 1685, the Huguenots had found themselves effectively disenfranchised, denied their rights to property and inheritance on French soil, and condemned for their religious practices [Baird, 1885]. In search of a place of tolerance for their reformist precepts, many of these Huguenot refugees made their way to St. Thomas, a colony that from its very establishment had emerged as a safe haven from strife and ethnic persecution [Knight, 2000]. But being latecomers, the Huguenots had found it difficult to acquire suitable lands on which to establish profitable plantations. As a result, when the decision was reached to expand the Danish West Indies and Guinea Company's colonial land holdings to include nearby St. John, a number of struggling Huguenots were among the first individuals willing to risk the harsh conditions of this unproven land [LD, 1722]. One of their number, a barber and surgeon by the name of Isaac Constantin, accompanied by his wife and nine-year-old daughter, left his failing cotton plantation on St. Thomas in 1721 and established himself on a low promontory overlooking a sandy cove on the North Shore of St. John: a place that for years to come would be known as Constantin's Bay [SJLL, 1728; Martfeldt, 1765].

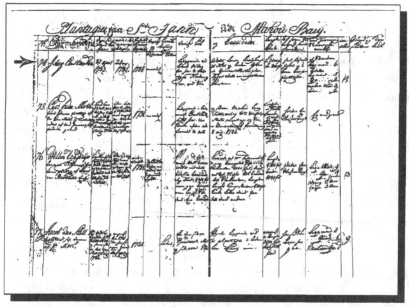

Extract from the first St. John tax rolls compiled in 1728, noting the plantation of Isacq [*sic*] Constantin, number 74
(Rigsarkivet, Denmark)

A typical West Indies sugar plantation of the early eighteenth century
(VIH&GRC library and archive, St. Thomas)

The Isaac Constantin Plantation, circa 1721 - 1779

Located a short distance east of the Annaberg factory complex, the fragmentary remains of an early period dwelling house, sugarworks, and enslaved workers' village are all that remain of the original Danish colonial period settlement established within the bounds of what was to become Estate *Annaberg*

Isaac Constantin's name first appears in records relating to St. John in a letter of report sent to the Danish West Indies and Guinea Company headquarters in Copenhagen by Governor Eric Bredal, dated July 15, 1722. In this report, it is stated that "Isaac Constantin, [is] a French refugee [who] resides on St. John. He had a small piece of land here [on St. Thomas], but on measuring his neighbors he has lost much of it and can no longer live from it" [LD, 1722].

On April 27, 1723, Constantin received a formal 'Land Letter' (deed) to his new St. John property [SJLL, 1728]. The St. Thomas tax rolls for that year confirm that Constantin, along with his wife Gierterud Sara Baset,[1] and their young daughter, Sarrie, were already in residence on their St. John plantation, and that the land was

---

[1] The surname of Isaac Constantin's wife also appears in documents during this era as "Moseth."

being worked by nine enslaved laborers -- one of which was listed as a 'maron' (runaway) [STLL, 1723]. It is, however, not until five years later, when tax accounts for St. John began to be compiled, that we are offered our first description of the size, location, and condition of the *Constantin* land holding. According to the 1728 St. John tax rolls, the *Constantin* plantation measured 3000 (Danish) feet long by 2000 feet broad, and was described as "lying by Water Lemon Bay, length running ESE and WNW and breadth East from Jac. V. Stell in Governor Moth's plantation, North and South to the manchineel trees by the seashore." The Constantins were still living on the property by this date, and the composition of the family was unchanged, but the number of enslaved laborers on the plantation had increased to twenty-four individuals: six fully taxable men, five male and three female 'bossaller' (newly imported Africans), three 'manqueron' (old or incapable of heavy labor), and six children. It was further stated that the *Constantin* parcel was a sugar plantation found to be in "mediocre" condition [SJLL, 1728].

No changes in the *Constantin* plantation were noted in the 1729 tax accounts, but by 1730 it was reported that a "sugarworks" had been constructed on the property. The presence of a works (or processing facility) marks an important turning point in the history of this plantation. After 1730 the Constantin family left St. John to once again take up residence on St. Thomas, leaving their plantation in the hands of a hired masterknegt (overseer), one Mr. Lestej [SJLL, 1730-31]. These occurrences clearly suggest that by that date the *Constantin* property had reached a state of development where stable productivity had finally been achieved.

Isaac Constantin died on St. Thomas in the fall of 1732. In the process of reconciling his estate, detailed inventories and appraisements of Constantin's home and plantation properties on St. Thomas and St. John were carried out. It is from the probate proceeding for his St. John plantation that we gain a rare glimpse into the composition of the *Constantin* property [STBP, 1732 - 1736]:

> Year 1732, the 4 December appeared interim town bailiff on St. Jan, Johan Reimer Soetman on the plantation of deceased Isak Constantyn [*sic*] for an honest registration and to appraise what is found on the plantation....

...A plantation here on St. John with a sugarworks, which length and breadth can be closer seen on the deed which has been shown to the St. Thomas probate court, appraised for:

Ps. 4500.0.0[2]

Animals

A stallion		40.0.0
A horse		50.0.0
A young stallion	30.0.0	
A mare		30.0.0
A donkey		10.0.0
A bull		40.0.0
A cow		24.0.0

Negros

A Negro man Fransisko, sugar cooker and bamba	200.0.0
ditto Jost.....	140.0.0
ditto Thonni....	145.0.0
ditto Sipio....	150.0.0
ditto Thoni, the old....	80.0.0
ditto Wille Maqueron....	60.0.0
A Negro woman Anna with a child, but the child given to Miss Sara [Constantin]....	60.0.0
A Negro boy Mingo....	100.0.0
A Negro Maron and Manqeron by name Samba, according to Madm. Constantyn's own saying worth....	50.0.0
A ditto Jacqva also Maron and by her reported for....	125.0.0...

[STBP, 1732 - 1736]

The probate proceedings for Isaac Constantin were interrupted in the fall of 1733 by the outbreak of the St. John slave

---

[2] Spanish silver eight reales, or pieces-of-eight, were a widely accepted standard monetary unit of this era.

rebellion. During the course of the uprising the dwelling house, boiling house, storage building, and slave village on the property were all burned, and the rum still badly damaged [STBP, 1732 - 1736].

Despite the damages wrought, by the spring of 1736, when Isaac Constantin's daughter, Sarrie, married Mads Larsen, a Danish immigrant from the town of Aalborg in Northern Jutland, thirteen enslaved laborers were once again at work on the plantation. And, by 1737, a sugarworks had been rebuilt on the site [SJLL, 1736-37; Ryberg, 1945].

Sarrie Constantin's husband, Mads Larsen, became the recorded owner of the *Constantin* plantation as his wife's guardian after their marriage in 1736 [SJLL, 1736]. But, with no children having been born of their union, after Sarrie's death sometime prior to the spring of 1746, the *Constantin* plantation came under administration by the court [Ryberg, 1945].

No tax records exist for St. John between 1740 and 1754, making it difficult to determine what transpired on the *Constantin* parcel over those years. When the tax records resume in 1755, it was recorded that Chancery (High Court) Counselor Jens Nielsen Kragh had become proprietor of the plantation [SJA, 1755]. As Kragh had previously been employed as Secretary for the Danish West Indies and Guinea Company, it is likely that he had been in possession of the property for some time previous to this date -- perhaps ever since it had been taken over for administration in 1746 [Larsen, 1940].

At this point there arises some question as to whether the industrial and residential complex of the *Kragh* plantation stood in the same location as the original *Constantin* settlement, or if it had been relocated during the years when the tax rolls are mute. It does seem, however, that Kragh, who did not hold free and clear title to the plantation, would have been unwilling to expend the required capital to improve and relocate the property's works during this period. Surface scatter observed throughout the Constantin complex, consisting of fragments of glass bottles and house wares, support this premise, and suggest that the site remained occupied until the third quarter of the eighteenth century. And indeed, a leap in the number of laborers on the plantation, from fifty-seven to ninety-two individuals reported in 1779, seems to mark the period when further development was undertaken on the property.

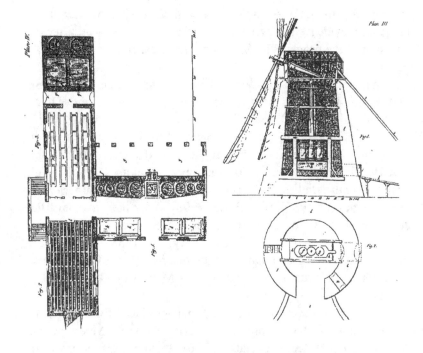

**Plans for a sugar factory and tower windmill
proposed by Peter L. Oxholm in 1797**

(Peter Lotharius Oxhlom, *De Dansk Vestindiske Oers Tilstand I Hanseende til
Population, Culture og Finance...* [Kobenhaven, Johan Frederik Schultz, 1797]).

The Rise and Fall of Estate Annaberg, circa 1779 - 1871

Situated on a coastal promontory approximately midway
between Annaberg Point and the mouth of Mary's Creek, the ruins of
the Annaberg sugar factory stand as an enduring historic landmark
amidst the fading cultural landscape of St. John's North Shore.
Although eighteenth-century maps and estate inventories indicate that
an earlier sugarworks and plantation residence were once located in
the same general location as the present factory structures, the ruins
that stand on *Annaberg* today represent the industrial complex of the
estate at the apex of its development just after the turn of the
nineteenth century.

As previously noted, it is not yet known at exactly what point
the residential and industrial heart of the former *Constantin* plantation

was relocated to the present Annaberg factory site, but available documentary evidence strongly suggests that it occurred well after the acquisition of the property by Salomon Zeeger Janzoon in 1758 [SJA, 1755-96].

Salomon Zeeger Janzoon was born on the Dutch island of St. Eustatius in 1729, the son of Jan Zeeger -- hence the Dutch patronymic identifier 'Janzoon" (Jan's-son) -- and Anna Maria Hassell. As a young man Zeeger immigrated to St. Thomas where in 1753 he married Anna deWindt, daughter of Johannes deWindt and Maria Battri: a prestigious union that speaks volumes for the high standing of both families in the rigid and exclusionary plantocracy of the eighteenth century [Hoff & Barta, 1998]. After their marriage the couple moved to St. John, where Zeeger had acquired a small cotton plantation on the outskirts of Cruz Bay. In 1758, the Zeegers expanded their St. John holdings with the purchase of the former *Constantin* sugar plantation in the island's Maho Bay Quarter [SJA, 1755-58].

Salomon Zeeger and Anna deWindt produced four daughters over the course of their union: Anna Maria, Elizabeth Mooy, Anna, and Adriana. Upon Zeeger's death in 1764, explicit instructions were left in his will that his daughters were to inherit the Maho Bay Quarter sugar plantation together, and that the property was to be cultivated to their common benefit [Knight, 1999; DVS, 1764]. Of the Zeeger daughters, only Anna appears to have died at an early age. The others all went on to wed men of wealth and prominence, who, upon marriage, became the joint owners of the former *Constantin* sugar plantation as their wives' guardians.

It was during this era that the first major push to expand the *Constantin* plantation took place. The oldest of the Zeeger daughters, Anna Maria, had married Peter deWindt, owner of the *Dewindtsberg* plantation that lay immediately west of the Zeeger heirs' property. It was through this union that a portion of *Dewindtsberg*, known as *Betty's Hope,* was parceled out and merged with the *Constantin* plantation [Hoff & Barta, 1998; PR, 1805]. This first expansion of the estate was initially carried out to increase the Zeegers' planting grounds, but at a later date it also provided a land link with the adjoining *Mary's Point* estate, which was purchased by the husband of Adriana Zeeger, John Shatford Jones, in 1789, and thereafter merged into the broader Zeeger heirs' holdings [SJA, 1789]. The third

Zeeger daughter, Elizabeth, married Benjamin Lind, a Crown employee who held the offices of Provisions Agent, Customs Officer, and Postmaster on St. John [Overman, 1974; Knight, 1999].

Together, John Shatford Jones, a savvy New York businessman and entrepreneur, Benjamin Lind, a well-connected government official, and Peter deWindt, an experienced local sugar planter of long West Indian heritage, possessed the knowledge, vision, and resources to transform the *Constantin* plantation into a large and productive sugar estate [Hoff & Barta, 1998; Knight, 1999]. And indeed, in 1779, under the reported proprietorship of Lind and Jones, the number of enslaved laborers on the property leaped from fifty-seven to ninety-two individuals: an increase of thirty-five workers, of whom, thirty-three were recorded as "capable" adults [SJA, 1779].

In a period when a healthy adult laborer was valued at from five to seven hundred pieces-of-eight, this sizable investment in manpower certainly coincided with a major initiative to boost production capabilities and increase the profitability of the property [MP, 1793]. It is likely, therefore, that it was at this time that the former Constantin site was abandoned, and a new residential and industrial complex was raised on a high promontory that was more centrally located within the estate's recently expanded acreage. This new facility was appropriately named *Annaberg* (Anna's-mountain) -- presumably in honor of the common matriarch of the Zeeger heirs on St. John, Anna deWindt Zeeger.

The relocation of the estate complex at this date may solve an intriguing anomaly that has long plagued researchers investigating the background of the *Annaberg* plantation. Why does a manuscript map of St. John prepared by Danish engineer Peter L. Oxholm between 1779 and 1780 not depict a sugar mill at *Annaberg*? The answer to this question could be that the new factory complex was still under construction at the time of Oxholm's survey, and the mill simply had not yet been built.[3]

---

[3] It should further be noted that an updated version of Oxholm's rendering of St. John published in 1800 indicates that an animal mill had been added to the *Annaberg* estate complex prior to that date. This map, however, was not current to the date of its publication, as it did not include the tower windmill that was under construction on the site as early as 1797.

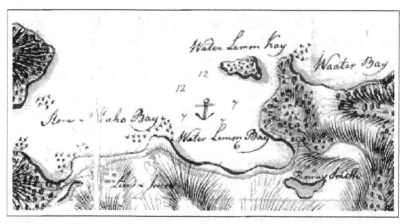

**Detail from Peter L. Oxholm's manuscript map of St. John, circa 1780,
noting the ownership of Lind & Jones**
[Rigsarkivet, Denmark]

The Zeeger heirs remained in at least partial control of the
Annaberg property until 1796, when all of the shares in the estate
were bought out by a wealthy St. Thomas merchant, ship owner, and
slave trader, James E. Murphy. In the year prior to his purchase of the
now merged *Annaberg (Constantin)*, *Betty's Hope* and *Mary's Point*
properties, Murphy had also acquired the adjoining *Smith Bay*
plantation, which he promptly renamed *Leinster Bay* after the Irish
province of his ancestry [SJA, 1796-98; MR, 1796-97].

Immediately following these acquisitions, construction began
on a state-of-the-art tower windmill and sugar factory on *Annaberg*,
which was to serve as a central processing facility for Murphy's
extensive sugar cane fields in the western section of his holdings [PR,
1805]. The plans for the new factory and windmill were based on
drawings that had been published that very year by Peter L. Oxholm,
with only minor modifications to adapt the structures to the steep
terrain of the site [Oxholm, 1797]. Concurrent with the construction
of the new factory, a grand estate house for Murphy's newly united
Annaberg and Leinster Bay plantation also began to take shape on a
formerly vacant hilltop overlooking Water Lemon Bay [SJA,
1797-1803; SJLBP, 1809].

By the turn of the nineteenth century the new Annaberg
factory complex and Leinster Bay estate house were near completion,
and James Murphy once again set out to expand his land holdings. In

1803, he acquired the *Munsbury* plantation that lay on *Annaberg's* southern boundary; and, in 1807, he purchased the *Brown Bay* estate east of Leinster Bay [SJA, 1803-07].

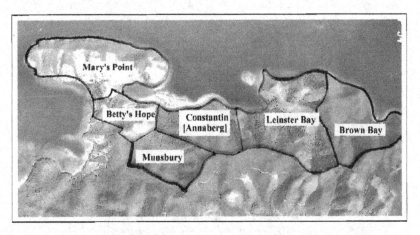

Approximate boundaries of the six estates associated with the *Annaberg* plantation circa 1807

On November 17, 1808, at the age of 51 years, James E. Murphy died on St. John and was buried on a prominent hilltop near his estate house overlooking Water Lemon Bay and the Annaberg factory.[4] At the time of his death, Murphy's *Annaberg and Leinster Bay* plantation comprised six formerly independent estates (made up of at least nine early colonial land grants), with a total land area of nearly 1,300 acres. Although the *Carolina* estate in Coral Bay was slightly larger in overall acreage, Murphy's 530 acres of cane fields made him the single largest sugar cane producer on St. John. He also controlled the island's largest labor force, with a total of 662 enslaved individuals -- sixty-one of whom were reported to be house servants and/or craftpersons [SJLBP, 1809; SJLL, 1728-39; SJA, 1809].

After the death of James Murphy a prolonged probate hearing took place, during which his properties were all appraised separately and apportioned out to service the claims of his many heirs and

---

[4] James Murphy's age is stated on his gravestone. Curiously, the date of death given on his monument, December 17, 1809, appears to be in error. According to his probate papers and other supporting documents Murphy's true date of death was November 17, 1808 [SJLBP, 1809; STLA, 1808].

creditors. In the process of reconciling the Murphy estate, the *Munsbury* parcel was sold, and *Brown Bay* reverted back to the mortgage holders, thus leaving the Murphy heirs with full title to the *Annaberg and Leinster Bay* plantation. Subsequently, *Leinster Bay* was given over to Murphy's son, Edward C. Murphy, and *Annaberg*, along with *Mary's Point* and *Betty's Hope*, became the property of his daughter, Mary Murphy Sheen. Although accounted for separately for tax and administrative purposes, *Annaberg* and *Leinster Bay* remained associated through common Murphy family ownership until 1863 [SJA, 1809-64].

It is from an appraisal of the *Annaberg* plantation compiled during James Murphy's probate proceedings that we gain our first detailed glimpse into the composition of the property at the very pinnacle of its development:

Appraisements over the Estate Annaberg
this day the 13th of October 1809

1 Windmill with leaded receiver, [with a] complete kitchen and oven under the gangway....	Ps. 15,000.
A complete cattle mill....	2,500.
1 New set of works with 8 Coppers & with a wall molasses cistern, and all the utensils....	30,000.
2 Stills of 250 gallons & one worm cistern and 2 Lead receivers....	4,000.
2 Three hundred gallon Butts....	80.
4 Butts of 200 gallons each	100.
1 Magass house, 60' by 24', and a mule pen with shade...	2,000.
1 Water cistern and wall spout 570 feet long and at an average 8 feet high....	1,600.
1 New necessary unfinished....	80.
1 Set of cane spouts, 1500 feet long....	400.
1 Truck....	20.
1 Stone wall 1330 feet long	

& about 4 feet high....	380.
65 Negro houses at 30 Ps [each]....	1,950.
27 Mules....	2,700.
1 Mare with a foal....	100.
130 Acres in cane at 300....	39,000.
20 Acres taken up in pasture and Negro buildings at Ps 50....	1,000.
90 Acres at a place called Mary's Point at Ps 50....	4,500.
20 Acres at a place called Mary's Point....	1,000.
[154 Slaves, all named and evaluated for]....	65,750.
Total Ps.	171,835.

Of the Estate formerly called
Dewindtsberg, or Betty's Hope,
there was showed to us
containing about 140 acres,
whereof:

40 in canes at Ps 200....	8,000.
90 in bush fit for cane land at Ps 75... .	6,750.
10 in bush fit for cane land at Ps 12 ½	125.
1 Dwelling house....	2000.
1 Kitchen and oven....	150.
1 Negro house....	50.
1 Set of Windmill timber framed, with cases, Gudgeons, Cotrells, Brasses, 30 gratings & 3 furnaces....	3,500.
Total Ps.	20,575.

[SJLBP, 1809]

After Mary Murphy Sheen and her husband Thomas died without issue, title to *Annaberg* reverted to the widow of Edward C. Murphy, Catharina Sheen Murphy in 1827 [SJA, 1827; SJLPD, 1827]. By the time of her inheritance of *Annaberg*, Catharina was married for a second time to Hans H. Berg, an individual of prominence, who was to rise to the position of Governor and Commandant of St. Thomas and St. John in 1853. As guardian for his wife and stepson (James Murphy's grandson, Edward Falkner Murphy), Berg retained title to *Annaberg* and *Leinster Bay* until his death in 1862 [Larsen, 1940; STBPP, 1834; STBEP, 1862].

Throughout most of this period *Annaberg* remained a profitable sugar estate with production levels exceeding 100,000 pounds of raw sugar per year as late as 1845. But growing soil depletion, a sagging colonial economy, and labor shortages after emancipation was achieved in 1848, all served to drive down production. In 1861, the year prior to Berg's death, *Annaberg's* sugar crop yielded less than five thousand pounds of raw sugar [SJRD, 1845-61].

After Governor Berg died, *Annaberg*, *Leinster Bay*, and *Mary's Point* were put up for auction individually. The *Mary's Point* property was purchased by Berg's former overseer George Francis, while *Annaberg* and *Leinster Bay* were purchased by a young Creole planter of mixed European and African descent, Abraham C. Hill. Hill, however, did not survive to take possession of the properties. Less than a year after his purchase of the estates, *Annaberg* and *Leinster Bay* were once again put up for auction, and on this occasion sold to Thomas Letsom Lloyd of Tortola [STBEP, 1862; SJCP, 1863].

For a time, Thomas Lloyd struggled to maintain sugar production on both *Annaberg* and *Leinster Bay*, but the catastrophic hurricane and earthquakes of 1867 were soon to end all hope for any further sugar production on those estates [SJRD, 1867-73]. With his factories in ruin, and his diminished cane fields rapidly reverting to bush, on April 13, 1871, Thomas Lloyd sold *Annaberg* and *Leinster Bay* to George Francis for the sum of $100, then quickly returned to Tortola to escape reprisals for the abandonment of his estates and laborers [STM, 1871; Low, 2001].

Sugar boiling house constructed by George Francis in 1874
(Photograph by D. Knight, November 2000)

The Era of Pasturing, Subsistence Agriculture, and Cottage Industry

George Francis was born enslaved on the *Annaberg* plantation. His name first appears in the earliest existing census for the property compiled in 1835, in which he was recorded as a thirteen-year old field laborer, baptized in the Moravian Church on June 21, 1822 [SJR, 1835].

Already a widower by age nineteen, George worked diligently to gain the respect of his fellow workers, as well as his influential master, Hans H. Berg. By the time the 1846 census was compiled, George Francis was among the most trusted of the estates' laborers, and by 1850 he had gained the position of "driver" (the leader of the work-gangs). Sometime in or about 1845, George Francis married Hester Dalinda, a young woman who had been born enslaved on the neighboring *Munsbury* plantation where she had lived all of her life. Secure in his new position as driver, Francis felt confident that a request to allow his wife to leave *Munsbury* and join him at *Annaberg* would not be refused. And indeed, a short time later Hester and her children, Peggy and Johannes, were all reported to be living at *Annaberg* [SJR, 1846, 1850, & 1855; SJLUC, 1850].

Over the course of the succeeding decades, George Francis found opportunities that in his youth must have seemed wholly unimaginable. In the 1860 census for *Annaberg*, Francis's position was listed as estate "overseer," and two years later he received clear and outright title to a 2-acre parcel of land on Mary's Creek by the will of his former owner, Hans H. Berg. But George Francis's ambitions did not stop there. Through hard work and frugality he managed to save enough money for a down-payment on the entire *Mary's Point* estate when it was auctioned off during the Berg probate reconciliation [STEP, 1862].

George Frances's wife, Hester, died a short time after their purchase of *Mary's Point*. The couple's possessions, itemized in Hester's probate inventory compiled on September 29, 1864, display the relative wealth the Francis family had attained by that date:

18 Head of Cattle
40 Sheep
3 Asses
2 Horses
1 Decked Boat 'The Ester of St. John'
1 Row Boat
2 Bedsteads with Bedding
2 Tables
1 Press
18 Chairs
1 doz. Plates, Knives, Forks, Spoons and Glasses
[SJCP, 1864]

Soon after Hester's death George Francis married for a third time to Lucy Ann Blyden. Together the couple lived on and worked the *Mary's Point* property, and in the 1870 census for the estate Francis had the gratification of listing his profession as "Planter." One year later he acquired the failing *Annaberg* and *Leinster Bay* estates from Thomas Lloyd, and immediately set out to renew sugar production on the properties.

George Francis died on St. John in 1875. He was the last individual to hold undivided title to the combined *Annaberg*, *Leinster Bay*, and *Mary's Point* estates. At the time of his death, Francis had recently completed the construction of a new sugar boiling house and horse mill on the isthmus between Mary's Creek and Francis Bay. It was the last sugar factory ever to be erected on St. John [STM, 1871-76].

After her husband's death, Lucy Blyden Francis found it difficult to cope with the finances of the estates, and in 1876 *Annaberg* and *Leinster Bay* were given over by adjudication to St. Thomas merchant Antoine Anduze [SJCP, 1875; SJA, 1876]. Anduze retained an overseer on his St. John properties, and converted the former crop lands to pasture. During this period, the deep valley behind Water Lemon Bay became the primary grazing area for Anduze cattle, and the lands associated with *Annaberg* appear to have been little utilized [STA, 1875-1899; SJCP, 1875-1899].

Annaberg and *Leinster Bay* remained in the hands of Antoine Anduze and his heirs until 1899. In that year, George Francis' son, Carl Emanuel Francis, along with his brother-in-law, Police Officer Henry Clen, were able to regain title to all of the *Annaberg, Leinster Bay,* and *Mary's Point* properties. Clen and his wife, Sophie Roseline Francis, took up residence in the former *Leinster Bay* estate house, while Carl Francis set up his household amidst the ruins of the Annaberg sugar factory, a place he christened *Francis' Castle* [STM, 1899, SJA, 1899].

Carl Francis, his wife Aimy and their family, lived amidst the ruins on *Annaberg* from 1900 until just prior to Carl's death in 1936. Like most St. John residents of this period, they lived a somewhat frugal and self-sufficient existence. They grew provision crops, grazed livestock, and produced quicklime and charcoal. Over the years Carl Francis rose to be a prominent and respected island figure. He served as the St. John representative to the Colonial Council (the local governing body prior to the establishment of the Virgin Islands Legislature), acted as Clerk and Lay Reader to the Nazareth Lutheran Congregation for over twenty years, and raised the first United States Flag over St. John in the transfer ceremonies held at the Cruz Bay Battery on April 15, 1917 [Moolenaar, 1992; Low & Valls, 1985].

Carl Francis sold the *Annaberg* estate to Herman O. Creque in 1935, and it was from the Creque heirs that the Jackson Hole Preserve purchased the property in 1954. *Annaberg* was officially turned over to the National Park Service in 1956 [Near, 2000].

Estate owner Carl Francis and family at *Annaberg*, circa 1919
(Above: Royal Library Photograph Collection, Copenhagen)
(Below: National Museum Photograph Collection, Copenhagen)

"The Sugar Cane, in its four different Stages"
(J. G. Steadman, *Narrative of an Expedition Against the
Revolted Negroes of Surinam,* [Amherst, Massachusetts,
Massachusetts University Press, 1971].)

Sugar Production on Estate Annaberg
(Historical Context)

Before proceeding with a discussion of how sugar was made
on the *Annaberg* plantation, it is necessary to briefly explore the
origins of sugar cane cultivation and the sugar production process.

A native to southern Asia, sugar cane has been nourishing
man since prehistoric times. It is not known for certain what culture
developed the technique of converting sugar cane juice into crystalline
sugar, but as the earliest known written reference to the process
appears in Sanskrit in about 500 B.C., historians have long credited
northern India as the place where sugar cane juice was first rendered

into a refined end-product. As with other tropical crops of Asian origin, such as bananas and mangos, sugar cane cultivation is believed to have slowly fanned outward from India into China and the Middle East over the course of many centuries. By A.D. 600 it had become well established in Persia, and within a century sugar cane had reached the shores of the eastern Mediterranean and North Africa where the first great economic sugar-boom occurred.

Although Europe had long been aware of sugar as a valued commodity of the eastern trade, it was not until the Crusades of the eleventh and twelfth centuries that western Europeans first encountered sugar cane under cultivation on the Mediterranean islands of Cyprus and Sicily. Attempts were soon made to introduce the crop further northward, but it was found that the properties of sugar cane were adversely affected by even the slightest frost. It therefore became apparent that the Mediterranean demarcated the far northern limit of sustainable sugar cane cultivation. For the next 400 years or so, the Mediterranean region continued to hold a near monopoly on the European sugar trade. But, as the age of Atlantic exploration dawned, sugar cane was among the first crops to be introduced into Europe's newly acquired tropical colonies -- first into the eastern Atlantic islands, and later into the West Indies and the Central and South American mainland. By 1450, sugar produced on Madeira had already begun to reach Europe, and by 1490 sugar from São Tomé (a Portuguese island possession in the Gulf of Guinea) had begun to enter northern markets as well. While the introduction of sugar cane into the eastern Atlantic islands surely had a negative impact on the long-established Mediterranean sugar trade, no single event would serve to more severely erode the Mediterranean's dominance of the industry than the proliferation of sugar cane throughout the New World.

Having quickly perceived the possibilities for sugar cane cultivation in the West Indies, Columbus brought sugar cane to the island of Hispañiola on his second voyage in 1493. In the early sixteenth century, subsequent Spanish expeditions carried the crop to Puerto Rico, Cuba, and Jamaica, then on to the American continent near Vera Cruz, Mexico, where it was reportedly under cultivation as early as 1525. But nowhere in the New World was sugar cane found to thrive better than in the humid environs of coastal Brazil. After King Manuel I of Portugal issued a royal order to introduce sugar cane cultivation into that region in 1516, the Pernambuco area quickly became the veritable epicenter of sugar production in the Americas. The long-depleted soils and drier conditions of the Mediterranean were no match for Brazil's optimum climate for sugar cane cultivation, or for its abundance of fertile, well-watered, arable lands, and the ready availability of enslaved laborers. The era of the Mediterranean's nearly one thousand-year dominance of the sugar industry rapidly drew to a close. By the end of the sixteenth century, the focus of sugar cane cultivation and sugar production had shifted across the Atlantic Ocean to the Americas; sugar cane had become nearly exclusively a New World crop.

While Spain and Portugal were the first countries to introduce sugar cane into the Americas, it was the Dutch who were largely responsible for its proliferation throughout the Lesser Antilles. Having learned the skills of sugar production during their takeover and occupation of Pernambuco between 1629 and 1654, savvy Dutch mercantilists set out to introduce the crop into the Eastern Caribbean, most notably on Barbados. By 1680, sugar was being produced on nearly all of the British- and French-held islands of the Caribbean, and sugar cane had become the dominant crop of the region [Ligon, 1673; Galloway, 1981; Watts, 1987].

It was during this period of rapid expansion of the West Indian sugar industry that Denmark first set out to establish a New World colony. Backed heavily by Dutch capital, in 1672 the Danish West Indies Company was finally successful in establishing a tenuous foothold on the island of St. Thomas. Soon after the arrival of the first Danish settlers, the colonists were joined by a small band of displaced Dutch planters and their families, who had been expelled by the British from the neighboring island of Tortola upon the outbreak of the Third Dutch War. With them, the Dutch refugees had not only brought sugar cane slips from the plantations that they had been forced to abandon on Tortola, but also the skills of sugar cane cultivation and a firsthand knowledge of the process for converting sugar cane juice into its valuable refined end-products: sugar, molasses, and rum [Knox, 1852; Westergaard, 1917; J.O. Bro-Jørgensen, 1966].

Despite the introduction of sugar cane into St. Thomas at the very outset of the colonizing effort, a lack of suitable land and the island's limited fresh water resources retarded the growth of the sugar

23

industry in the Danish colony. As late as 1715, only about one-third of St. Thomas's plantations were planted in sugar cane, and no more than thirty-two properties were reported to have sugar processing facilities [STLL, 1715]. It was largely in the hopes of expanding the Danish West Indies Company's share in the increasingly profitable sugar trade that the decision was finally reached to extend Denmark's colonial holdings to the neighboring island of St. John. In 1718, when Governor Bradel first laid out a set of guidelines for the occupation of that island, one of the six requirements was that a sugarworks was to be erected on each plantation within five years on penalty of the confiscation of the property [BD, 1718]. While it was later realized that not all of the land holdings on St. John were suitable for sugar cane cultivation and the order was never enforced, any planter with the necessary capital and appropriate location was clearly encouraged to do so. [SJLL, 1728]. It was not, however, until the turbulent decades that mark the turn of the nineteenth century, that St. John's low yield plantations began to be merged and developed into large scale agro-industrial sugar estates.

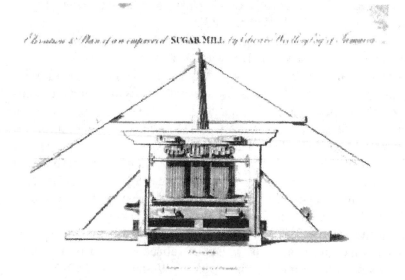

An animal driven sugar mill used throughout the colonial period
(VIH&GRC Library and Archive, St. Thomas)

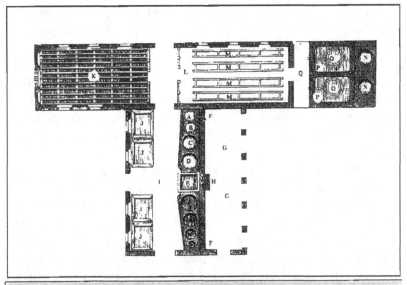

A) Teache, or fourth copper	J) Cooling pans
B) Third kettle, or third copper	K) Curing house
C) Second kettle, or second copper	L) Still house
D) The grand copper	M) Trestles to support the
E) Clarifier	fermentation butts
F) Firing holes of the furnace	N) Pot-stills
G) Firing trench	O) Worm, or condensation coil
H) Chimney	P) Worm cistern
I) Boiling house	Q) Receiver

A Closer Look at the Annaberg Factory Complex
and the Sugar Production Process

      Toward the close of the eighteenth century, the North American struggle for independence, combined with the rising populist fervor of the French Revolution, engulfed the entire western world in turmoil. Upon the French National Convention's declarations of war against the British and Dutch in February 1793, and Spain in March of the same year, commerce in the neutral ports of the Danish West Indies began to flourish; St. Thomas soon emerged as a regional hub for the hyperactive commerce of conflict. With France's wealthiest sugar producing colony of Saint Domingue crippled by chaos, and her slave-owning planters of the Lesser Antilles in league with the British against the radical Jacobins of the motherland, France was effectively stripped of her dominance over the West Indian sugar trade [Stein, 1988; Rogozinski, 1992]. As war and revolt wore on, the supply of West Indies goods became increasingly constricted and sugar prices soared. In the animated entrepot of Charlotte Amalie, locally produced muscovado sugar rose in value from seven to nine dollars per hundredweight in 1795, to fifteen dollars by the close of the year 1797, while rum reached the startling figure of one dollar per gallon [Nissen, 1838].

With sugar prices at an all-time high, wealthy capitalists in London and Liverpool were quick to take advantage of the void left in the sugar market by the declining fortunes of the French. Through their local attorneys (known in England as factors), they began to extend liberal lines of credit on sugar futures for the purchase, expansion, and modernization of sugar plantations throughout the Danish West Indies. Many planters borrowed heavily against their estates and future production during this period, and while some were able to service their debts and reap considerable fortunes from their properties, others were less fortunate: their bankrupt estates falling into the hands of British creditors [STLA, 1808-10; SCR, 1807-26; Pares, 1950].

In 1795, at the very height of this turbulent period of high valuations and wild speculation, a wealthy St. Thomas-based merchant and ship owner, James E. Murphy, purchased the floundering *Smith Bay* (aka: *Leinster Bay*) plantation on St. John, and soon after began to methodically acquire shares in the neighboring *Annaberg* estate, with its associated properties of *Betty's Hope* and *Mary's Point*. By 1796, Murphy had attained his goal of sole proprietorship, and under the supervision of his trusted plantation manager, Owen Sheridan, set out to transform his new holdings into what was to become the largest sugar-producing plantation in the history of St. John [MR, 1795-97; PR, 1805; SJA; 1795-1809].

The plantation that James Murphy developed was far from characteristic for the island of St. John in this, or any period, resembling more in size and scope of operations the sprawling sugar estates of St. Croix or Barbados. Clearly Murphy did not envision his properties as a group of individual plantations, but as a single, broad and integral land holding on which specific areas of endeavor were developed to maximize efficiency and take advantage of the specific resources present in that section of his estate. On a breezy hilltop with panoramic vistas overlooking the extent of his property and its approaches by land and sea, Murphy constructed a stately and well-fortified mansion house. And, along the shore of the estate's sheltered deep water anchorage on Water Lemon Bay, a center for support activities was established, consisting of warehouses, boat sheds, a lime kiln, blacksmith and carpentry shops, and a complete sugarworks to process the cane grown on the eastern section of the plantation. But, if there was a crowning jewel in Murphy's plan, one project that was to be the most costly and ambitious of all his undertakings, it was the construction of a new and modern sugar factory on the former site of the Annaberg sugarworks: a complex that would serve as the central processing facility for the nearly two hundred acres of sugar cane that stretched across the landscape on the western section of the estate [PR, 1805; SJLBP, 1809].

The sugar factory complex that Murphy constructed on *Annaberg* was based on a proposed plan by Peter L. Oxholm, published in 1797 -- the year after Murphy's purchase of the *Annaberg* estate [SJLBP, 1809]. While Oxholm's tower windmill design appears atypical, his proposed 'T' shaped factory building, with its double battery of kettles and two stills, was truly innovative. In an effort to bring the capability of the boiling house up to a level of productivity that would match, or exceed, the windmill's capacity to provide cane juice to the factory's receivers, the Oxholm plan brought under one roof the processes of boiling cane juice down into syrup, the cooling of the syrup into crystalline raw sugar, the extraction and collection of molasses from that sugar, and the distillation of rum from a mixture of molasses and fermented residue of the sugar boiling process. The plan effectively increased output by maximizing the efficiency of a series of related, successive procedures by way of ordered proximity -- a concept that would come to be embraced in most areas of manufacture during the industrial revolution, and might well be seen as the forerunner to the assembly line made famous by Henry Ford a century later [Oxholm, 1797; Linvald, 1967]. It should be noted, however, that Oxholm's design was better suited to the flat or moderately hilly topography of St. Croix, and the Annaberg sugar factory required numerous adaptations of the plan to conform to the mountainous terrain of St. John. It is here that the ingenuity of the individual, or individuals, who were responsible for those modifications shines through, as it is the efficient use of the topography that stands out as the most unique and distinguishable feature of the Annaberg sugarworks.

To efficiently process the amount of sugar cane grown on the expanded *Annaberg* estate, James Murphy constructed a new and complete factory complex on the site where the previous sugarworks described in the 1793 property inventory had stood. The new Annaberg works utilized two mills for the extraction of juice from the cane stalks: an animal mill and a windmill. Before construction of the windmill could proceed, it was necessary to create enough level ground on which to erect the tower. To accomplish this, a massive retaining wall was built and back-filled downslope to the north and east of the site, while the western side of the flat was retained by the far walls of the property's animal mill. Although the base of the windmill was smaller in circumference than that of the rotunda for the animal mill, a somewhat larger level area was needed for the windmill in order to accommodate both the sloping gangway that led up to the mill's main opening, and the broad sweep of the tail-tree that controlled the windmill turret so that its blades could be adjusted into, or away from the prevailing winds.

South of the mills, a large 'T' shaped building was erected to house the plantation's primary processing facility. In the stem of the 'T', just opposite and downslope of the animal mill, was a long single-story room known as the **boiling house**, where the freshly squeezed sugar juice was condensed into a thick syrup [I].[5]

Situated along the west wall of the boiling house was a raised platform that held two **batteries** of kettles comprised of four kettles each called the **boiling bench** [A, B, C, & D]. These kettles, known also as **coppers**, were laid out in descending order of size on either side of a large receiving tank called the **clarifier** [E].

Heat for the boiling bench was provided by two **furnaces** [F]: one for each battery of kettles. The furnaces were stoked from an area on the outside of the west wall of the boiling house known as the **firing trench** [G]. Oxholm's plan called for the use of a furnace design known as a **Jamaica train**. In the Jamaica train, one fire, lit and maintained under the smallest and hottest pot in the boiling bench,

[5] **NOTE:** All bracketed letters encountered in the following text relate to the ground plan of the Oxholm sugar factory found on page 25 of this section.

the **teache** [A], was used to heat the entire battery; while the temperature of the individual kettles was controlled by a series of damper doors located along the length of the firing trench. Smoke from the furnaces was expelled by way of a tall external **chimney** [H], situated in-between the two batteries of kettles opposite the clarifier.

Cross section of a 'Jamaica train furnace
(Detail from: Diderot, 1752 [Reprinted 1959)]

Along the east wall of the interior of the boiling house, directly across from the boiling bench, was an area reserved for the placement of a series of shallow, lead-lined **cooling pans** [J], in which the freshly cooked syrup was periodically turned, or raked, as it hardened into crystalline sugar.

Because the Annaberg sugar factory was built on a steep slope, the southern end of the structure that formed the head of the 'T' stood three stories tall. In the top wooden loft or attic story, were the quarters of the plantation's overseer and under-overseer. On the second story, which was level with the floor of the boiling house, the room in the western wing was used as a storeroom and staging area, where the crystallized raw sugar was packed into barrels with holes drilled into one end [above L]. From there, the barrels were rolled into the room on the opposite side of this wing called the **curing house** [K], which had a floor made of open grating. Under this grating was a second sloped floor, with channels leading to an opening situated directly above the **molasses cistern** that stood on the ground floor. The freshly packed barrels of sugar were placed upright on the grating with the holed ends facing downward. Over a period of roughly two to three weeks the barrels were allowed to drain in this manner, while the molasses separated from the sugar crystals and collected in the tank below. Once fully drained, the barrels were sealed and the sugar was conveyed to a warehouse on the bay to await shipping. Meanwhile, the molasses that had been collected in the cistern on the ground floor under the curing house was drawn off and barreled in the open area at the east side of the room [below K]. Some of the molasses was tightly sealed and sent to the warehouse along with the sugar for export, but a portion (depending on the market price of molasses and rum) was transported to the **still house** to be used in the production of rum [L].

On the floor of the still house were mounted heavy timber trestles that elevated and supported large wooden fermentation tanks known as **butts** [M]. It is known from an inventory of the *Annaberg* plantation that two 300-gallon and four 200-gallon butts stood in the still house during this period. Outside, on the far western end of the still house wing, stood a **worm cistern** (shown in the Oxholm plan as two cisterns) [P], and beyond that were two furnaces over which copper **pot-stills** were mounted [N]. A portion of fermented liquid made from a mixture of water, molasses, and skimmings (or skummimgs), taken off the top of the boiling cane juice, was drawn off from the butts and placed into the stills. When boiled, the mixture turned to steam and rose into a collector, from where it was directed into a series of tubular coils submerged in cool water called the **worm** [O]. As the steam cooled, it condensed into liquid alcohol (rum), which exited the end of the coil through a pipe into a shallow trough at the base of the worm cistern called a **receiver** [Q].

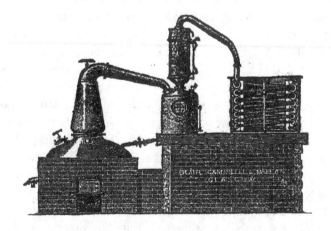

A nineteenth century rum still
(von Scholten Collection, Baa Library, St. Thomas)

It is here in the Annaberg distillery that an ingenious adaptation of the Oxholm plan is most apparent. In the hot and drought-prone islands of the Lesser Antilles, the production levels of a distillery were limited by a facility's ability to access cool water to create efficient condensation. If cool water was not continually added to the worm cistern during the distillation process, the steam going through the coils would heat the water and the still would have to be shut down while the worm cistern cooled [Anon., 1785]. To overcome this problem on *Annaberg*, a 570-foot elevated aqueduct was constructed to carry cool water to the worm cistern from a spring-fed holding tank located uphill to the southeast of the factory. As the water in the worm cistern warmed, it was drawn off and either directed through a channel into the boiling house, where it was used for rinsing out the sugar kettles, or sent directly into the still house to refill the butts for a new round of fermentation. Either way, the warm water from the worm cistern always ended up in the fermentation butts, as whatever amount was used for cleaning the kettles was afterwards ladled into the skimming channel on the front of the boiling bench that led down into the still house.

How Sugar Was Made at the Annaberg Factory

At *Annaberg* sugar cane was cut in the fields and conveyed to the mills by various means. Wooden channels were used to "shoot" the sugar cane downhill from the fields in the upland areas of the plantation, and a "windlass" was used to hoist sugar cane up from the fields in the valley below the factory. But, as on most properties, the majority of the sugar cane was brought to the mills by cart.

Once near the mill the cane stalks were cut short, bundled, and carried by hand to the grinders. All canes were passed through the mill's grinding machinery twice, after which the spent stalks, called **magass,** were carried away to a drying shed for later use as fuel for the furnaces of the boiling house.

Juice from the crushed cane ran out of the bottom of the grinders into a large vessel known as the **receiver**. The flow of the juice collected in the receiver could be controlled. When fresh juice was needed in the factory it was released from the receiver into a trough or pipe that led downhill into a tank in the factory known as a

clarifier (at different dates the Annaberg boiling house might have had as few as one, or as many as three clarifiers).

A tower windmill and sugar factory of the nineteenth century
(Barbados Museum and Historical Society Library, St. Michael, Barbados)

The clarifier, which generally held between 300 and 400 gallons, was situated on the boiling bench in a position where its contents were heated but never boiled. To the juice in the clarifier was added a temper, such as lime powder, a vegetable alkali, or the ashes of certain woods, and as the mixture warmed impurities attached to the temper and rose to the surface as scum. Unlike the froth that was formed in the pots at a later stages of the boiling process, scum from the clarifier could not be used in the fermentation butts for the distillation of rum. It was, however, collected and made into slop for animal feed.

The cane juice remained in the clarifier for approximately an hour while impurities collected on top. Once ready for boiling, the juice was let out of the clarifier by way of a cock or siphon into the largest boiling pot on the bench known as the **grand copper**. As the juice in the grand copper boiled, a thick frothy scum formed on the top. This residue was used in the same manner as the scum from the clarifier, while skimmings from the final three kettles were taken off and placed in a channel that ran down the front of the boiling bench into the still house where they were put in the fermentation butts. When the contents of the grand copper had been reduced through evaporation by roughly half, the now somewhat thicker juice was quickly ladled into the next copper in the battery, and the grand copper was refilled from the clarifier.

Scene in a nineteenth-century boiling house
(Barbados Museum and Historical Society Library, St. Michael, Barbados)

As boiling and skimming continued in the **second and third coppers,** the juice became increasingly reduced. At this stage, it was often necessary to add lime-water to the coppers in order to facilitate further tempering and dilute the juice's thickness.

Finally, the thickened juice was ladled into the fourth and hottest kettle called the **teache,** where the final stage of evaporation was carried out. By this point the juice had become a heavy syrup, and it was tested in cold water for coagulation. When deemed ready, the syrup was rapidly ladled into shallow, lead-lined boxes called **cooling pans**. The act of removing the juice from the teache at the proper moment before the sugar burned, but after the point when it would crystallize upon cooling, was called **striking**, and it was amongst the most critical procedures in the sugar production process.

Cooling pans were usually 7 feet long by 5 feet wide and held roughly 1,600 pounds of sugar. Once in the cooling pan the cane syrup gradually hardened into a coarse mass of crystals in a thick brown residue called **molasses**. As the crystals formed, they were constantly raked in order to separate the grains and prevent the sugar from clumping. Once the sugar was sufficiently cooled, it was transported to the **curing house** where the process of draining off the molasses was carried out.

Sugar produced in this manner, known as **muscovado**, was still quite dark in color. The refining of muscovado into white sugar was not allowed in the Danish West Indies. That right was reserved for the large and powerful sugar refineries in Denmark. Rum, which was made with byproducts from the sugar production process, was the only truly refined end-product exported from the Annaberg factory during the colonial period.

Hogsheads of sugar headed for export
(VIH&GRC Library and Archive, St. Thomas)

Nineteenth-Century Modifications to
the Annaberg Factory Complex

It must be stressed that the preceding sections have sought to portray the primary processing facility on the *Annaberg* estate as it was at the time of its construction between 1797 and 1805. But, as evidenced by even a cursory inspection of the ruins that stand on the site today, the Annaberg complex has undergone any number of modifications over the years -- the most recent being the large-scale stabilization efforts carried out by the National Park Service in the latter half of the twentieth century.

Inventories for the estate indicate that sometime prior to 1863 the boiling bench in the Annaberg factory was converted to a single battery of four kettles, with perhaps as many as three built-in clarifying tanks. Presumably at the same time the distillery was reduced to one pot-still. These modifications are represented by the configuration encountered on the site today. It is possible that this down-sizing of production capabilities occurred as early as the end of the first quarter of the eighteenth century, when tax records indicate that the amount of sugar cane under cultivation on the plantation plummeted from 200 to less than 90 acres, and the enslaved population dropped from 180 to 155 individuals [SJA, 1819-25]. While the exact dates of any of the alterations to the Annaberg factory during the Danish colonial period remain uncertain, it is clear that after emancipation was achieved in 1848, labor shortages and falling sugar prices had made it no longer economically feasible to run and maintain the facility at anything close to its original levels of production. Although sugar continued to be made at *Annaberg* until the devastating year of 1867, production had long been erratic at best, and the cane-sugar industry as a whole had been in general decline since the end of the first quarter of the nineteenth century [SJRD, 1846-70; STA, 1803-1915]. By the time a census was compiled on St. John in the fall of 1870, the Annaberg factory complex lay totally abandoned, its outdated equipment and processing facilities damaged beyond all hope of a profitable resumption of production. No organized large-scale sugar production, or attempts to modify the structures on the site for alternative industries, has taken place at the Annaberg factory complex since that date.

The Annaberg windmill tower, circa 1959
(Photograph by Dr. George H. H. Knight)

Postscript

It is intriguing to note that if it were not for one obscure document we may never have known the dates, or which of the many owners was the individual responsible for the construction of the imposing Annaberg sugar factory complex. Buried amidst the voluminous records relating to the Danish West Indies colony in the Danish National Archives in Copenhagen, was found a single sheet of tabulations pertaining to the enslaved population on *Annaberg* in 1805. In a blank space at the bottom of the page labeled "Observations," James Murphy's plantation manager, Owen Sheridan, wrote in a cramped, but legible script:

> *"On this estate is a wind mill, cattle mill, a large & convenient set of works, a magass house, a mule pen with sheds, all built since 1797..."* [PR, 1805].

Sources

BIBLIOGRAPHY
(alphabetical by surname)

Anonymous, *Letters To A Young Planter; Or, Observations On The Management Of A Sugar Plantation* [written on the island of Grenada] (London, J. Strachan, 1785).

Charles W. Baird, *History Of The Huguenot Emigration To America*, Vol. I & II (New York, Dodd, Mead & Company, 1885).

F. W. N. Bayley, *Four Years Residence In The West Indies* (London, William Kidd, 1830).

Betsy Bradley and Elizabeth Rezende, *Captured In Time: 1919* (St. Croix, VI, Island Perspectives, 1987).

Israel Bowman, *Hints To Young Barbados-Planters* (Barbados, Israel Bowman, 1857).

J.O. Bro-Jørgensen, *Vore Gamle Tropekolonier, Dansk Vestindien Indtil 1755*, vol.1 (Fremand, Denmark, 1966).

N. P. Burgh, *A Treatise On Sugar Machinery* (London, E. & F. N. Spon, 1863).

Noel Deerr, *The History Of Sugar* (London, Chapman & Hall Ltd., 1949).

Denis Diderot, *L'Encyclopédie, ou Dictionnaire Raisonné des Sciences, des Arts et des Métiers* (New York, Dover Publications, Inc., 1959 [First published in 1752]).

Isaac Dookhan, *A History of the British Virgin Islands* (Essex, Caribbean University Press, 1975).

Isaac Dookhan, *A History of the Virgin Islands of the United States* (Jamaica, Canoe Press, 1994).

J. W. Evens, *The Sugar-Planter's Manual, Being A Treatise On The Art Of Obtaining Sugar From the Sugar-Cane* (Philadelphia, Lee & Blanchard, 1848).

Harry A. Frank, *Roaming Through The West Indies* (New York, Blue Ribbon Books, 1920).

J. H. Galloway, *The sugar cane industry: An historical geography from its origins to 1914* (Cambridge, Cambridge University Press, 1989).

R. Greenwood and S. Hamber, *Emancipation to Emigration* (London, Macmillan Education Ltd., 1980).

David W. Knight, *A Brief History of the Cinnamon Bay Estate on St. John in the Danish West Indies, 1718 - 1917* (St. Thomas, USVI, Little Nordside Press, 1999).

David W. Knight, *Into the Light; The Enigmatic History of Water Island in the Danish West Indies, 1672 - 1917* (St. Thomas, USVI, Little Nordside Press, 2000).

David W. Knight, *The Story of Estate Lindholm, 1718 - 1917* (St. Thomas, USVI, Little Nordside Press, 1999).

John P. Knox, *A Historical Account of St. Thomas in the Danish West Indies* (New York, Charles Scribner, 1852).

Kay Larsen, *Guvernører Residenter, Kommandanter og Chefer* (Copenhagen, Denmark, Arthur Jensen Forlag, 1940).

Lief Calundann Larsen, *The Danish Colonization of St. John, 1718-1733* (St. Thomas, The V. I. Resource Management Cooperative, 1986).

Florence Lewisohn, *Diverse Information on The Romantic History of St. Croix From the Time of Columbus until Today* (Virgin Islands, St. Croix Landmarks Society, 1964).

Richard Ligon, *A True & Exact History Of the Island of Barbadoes* (London, Frank Cass Publishers, 1970 [First printed London, 1657]).

Steffen Linvald, *Sukker og Rom* (Copenhagen, Foreningen Dansk Vestindien, 1967).

Ruth Hull Low & Rafael Valls, *St. John Backtime, Eyewitness Accounts from 1718 to 1956* (St. John, U.S. Virgin Islands, Eden Hill Press, 1985).

Ruth Hull Low, *St. John Voices, 1717 - 1975* (Chillmark, Massachusetts, Eden Hill Press, to be published).

Christian Martfeldt, *Samlinger om de Danske Vestindiske Öer St. Croix, St. Thomas, St. Jan,* Vol. III. (Denmark, Manuscript in the Rigsarkivet, circa 1765).

Ruth Moolenaar, *Profiles Of Outstanding Virgin Islanders* (Virgin Islands, Department of Education, 1992).

Henry Morton, *Danish West Indian Sketch Book and Diary, 1843 - 1844* (Copenhagen, Dansk Vestindisk Selskab & St. Croix Landmark Society, 1975).

Colonel Charles Theodor Overman, *The Henrietta Estate (Hacienda Enriqueta) and The Overman and Lind Who Owned It from 1827 to 1882* (British Columbia, Canada, Col. C. T. Overman, 1974).

Arthur P. Newton, *The European Nations in the West Indies, 1493 - 1688* (London, A & C Black Ltd., 1933).

John P. Nissen, *Reminisences Of A 46 Years' Residence In The Island Of St. Thomas, In The West Indies* (Nazareth, PA, Senseman & Co., 1838).

Peter Lotharius Oxholm, *De Dansk Vestindiske Oers Tilstand I Hanseende til Population, Culture og Finance...* (Kobenhaven, Johan Frederik Schultz, 1797).

Pierre J. Pannet (Translated and Edited by Aimery Caron and Arnold R. Highfield), *Report on the Execrable Conspiracy Carried Out by the Amina Negroes on the Danish Island of St. Jan in America 1733* (U. S. Virgin Islands, Antilles Press, 1984).

Richard Pares, *A West-India Fortune* (London, Longmans, Green and Co., 1950).

George Richardson Porter, F. R. S., *The Nature And Properties Of Sugar Cane* (London, Smith, Elder and Co., 1843).

Jan Rogoziński, *A Brief History Of The Caribbean* (New York & Oxford, Facts On File, 1992).

Hugo Ryberg, *A List of Names of Inhabitants of the Danish West Indies from 1650 - ca, 1825* (Copenhagen, Published by Compiler, 1945).

Robert Louis Stein, *The French Sugar Business in the Eighteenth Century,* (Baton Rouge, Louisiana State University Press, 1988).

Jens Vibæk, *Vore Gamle Tropekolonier, Dansk Vestindien 1755 - 1848*, vol. 2 (Denmark, Fremand, 1966).

David Watts, *The West Indies, Pattern of Development, Culture and Environmental Change since 1492* (United Kingdom, Cambridge University Press, 1987).

Waldemar Westergaard, *The Danish West Indies Under Company Rule* (New York, The Macmillen Company, 1917).

PERIODICALS
(alphabetical by publication)

Henry B. Hoff, F.A.S.G. and The Rev. F. Kenneth Barta, "De Windt Families of the West Indies, Descendants of Lieven De Windt of St. Thomas," *The Genealogist*, Vol. 10, #2 [Utah, Association for the Promotion of Scholarship in Genealogy, Ltd., 1998].

Don Near, "100 Years at Annaberg Plantation," *St. John Times*, November 2000 [St. John, June Bell Barlas, Editor and Publisher, 2000].

PRIMARY SOURCES
(alphabetical by abbreviation)

[DVS] Danish Chancery, East and West Indies Records, 1688 - 1799 (Rigsarkivet, Denmark).

[LD] West Indies and Guinea Company Archives, Letters and Documents, 1674 - 1754 (Rigsarkivet, Denmark).

[MP] Record Group 55, St. John Mortgage-protocols 1766 - 1821 (U. S. National Archives II, College Park, Maryland).

[MR] Record Group 55, St. Thomas - St. John Mortgage Registers, 1776 - 1806 (U. S. National Archives II, College Park, Maryland).

[PR] West Indies Local Archives, Plantation Reports, 1797 - 1805 (Rigsarkivet, Denmark).

[SJA] Central Management Archives, West Indies Audit Registers for St. John, 1755 - 1915 (Rigsarkivet, Denmark).

[SCR] Records of the Royal West Indian Superior Court, Deed and Encumbrance-books, 1807-1826 (Office of the Recorder of Deeds, St. Croix, Virgin Islands).

[SJCP] Record Group 55, Case Papers Before the St. John Probate Court, (U. S. National Archives II, College Park, Maryland).

[SJLD] West Indies Local Archives, St. John Landfoged, Diverse Correspondence, 1828 - 1856 (Rigsarkivet, Denmark).

[SJLL] West Indies and Guinea Company Archives, St. John Land Lists, 1728 - 1733 & 1736-1739 (Rigsarkivet, Denmark).

[SJLM] West Indies Local Archives, St. John Landfoged, Mortgage Protocols, 1767 - 1791, (Rigsarkivet, Denmark).

[SJLBP] West Indies Local Archives, St. John Landfoged, Bailiffs' Protocols, 1789 - 1913 (Rigsarkivet, Denmark).

[SJLP] West Indies Local Archives, St. John Landfoged, Probate Sessions Protocol, 1758 - 1775 (Rigsarkivet, Denmark).

[SJLPD] West Indies Local Archives, St. John Landfoged, Probate-documents, 1778 - 1859 (Rigsarkivet, Denmark).

[SJLPL] West Indies Local Archives, St. John Landfoged, Probate-letters, 1783 - 1806 (Rigsarkivet, Denmark).

[SJLPP] West Indies Local Archives, St. John Landfoged, Probate-protocols, 1741 - 1823 (Rigsarkivet, Denmark).

[SJLRA] West Indies Local Archives, St. John Landfoged, Probate Registrations and Appraisements, 1797 - 1807 (Rigsarkivet, Denmark).

[SJLRAP] West Indies Local Archives, St. John Landfoged, Probate Registrations and Appraisement Protocols, 1835 - 1882 (Rigsarkivet, Denmark).

[SJLRTP] West Indies Local Archives, St. John Landfoged, Registrations, Appraisements, Sessions and Testament Protocols, 1807 - 1826 (Rigsarkivet, Denmark).

[SJLS] West Indies Local Archives, St. John Landfoged, Land-matters, 1811 - 1845 (Rigsarkivet, Denmark).

[SJLUC] West Indies Local Archives, St. John Landfoged, Unarranged Correspondence, 1851 - 1875 (Rigsarkivet, Denmark).

[SJR] Central Management Archives, Registers for St. John, 1835 - 1911 (Rigsarkivet, Denmark).

[SJRD] West Indies Local Archives, St. John Landfoged, Register of Duties, 1845 - 1873 (Rigsarkivet, Denmark).

[STBEP] West Indies Local Archive, St. Thomas Byfoged, Executor Probates, 1778 - 1868 (Rigsarkivet, Denmark).

[STBP] West Indies Local Archive, St. Thomas Byfoged, Probate Protocol for Planters, 1728 - 1736, Ltr. G (Rigsarkivet, Denmark).

[STBPP] West Indies Local Archive, St. Thomas Byfoged, Probate Sessions Protocols, 1817 - 1893 (Rigsarkivet, Denmark).

[STEP]West Indies Local Archive, St. Thomas Byfoged, Executors' Probates, 1778 - 1868 (Rigsarkivet, Denmark).

[STLA] CO 259, piece 4, St. Thomas Loan Accounts, 1808 - 1810 (Public Records Office, Kew, United Kingdom).

[STLL] West India and Guinea Company, St. Thomas Land Lists, (1686) 1688-1754 (Rigsarkivet, Denmark).

[STM] St. Thomas / St. John Mortgage and Deed Registers, NA (Office of the Recorder of Deeds, St. Thomas, Virgin Islands).

[STMC] Central Management Archives, West Indies Journals, Health-services, 1817 - 1916 (Rigsarkivet, Denmark).

[STTRB] West Indies and Guinea Company Archives, St. Thomas Report Books (Rigsarkivet, Denmark).

[VIC] Department of Commerce, Record Group 29, Records of the Bureau of Census 1920, Virgin Islands [compiled in 1917] (U. S. National Archives, Washington, DC).

Further Reading
A Select Bibliography of Reports and Published Sources
With References to Estate Annaberg

REPORTS

Mark Barnes, *National Historic Landmark Nomination for Annaberg Plantation and School* (Washington DC, United States Department of the Interior, National Park Service, Unpublished Preliminary Draft, 2001).

David M. Brewer & Susan Hammersten, *Archeological Overview and Assessment, Virgin Islands National Park, St. John, U.S. Virgin Islands* (Florida, Southeast Archeological Center, National Park Service, Tallahassee, 1988).

Frederik Gjessing, *St. John Sites Report 1981-82* (Virgin Islands, Virgin Islands National Park, 1982).

Frederik C. Gjessing, *The Tower Windmill For Grinding Sugar Cane* (Virgin Islands, Bureau of Libraries Museums & Archaeological Services, Department of Conservation & Cultural Affairs, 1977).

Charles E. Hatch Jr., *Virgin Islands National Park. St. John Island ("The Quiet Place") With Special Reference to Annaberg Estate, Cinnamon Bay Estate* (Washington, DC, National Park Service, 1972).

Regina M. Leabo, "Investigations Conducted At The Slave Village On The Annaberg Plantation, St. John, U.S. Virgin Islands", *SEARCHING...*, First Quarter 1997 (Florida, National Park Service, Southeast Archaeological Center, 1997).

Judy Shafer, *Archeological Monitoring of the Northshore Road, Phase II* (Colorado, Denver Service Center, National Park Service, 1993)

Kenneth S. Wild, Elizabeth A. Horvath, Douglas T. Potter, Andrea C. Repp, *1987-89 Archeological Investigations Conducted Along The North Shore Road, St. John, U.S. Virgin Islands* (Florida, National Park Service, Southeast Archeological Center, Tallahassee).

Kenneth S. Wild, Jr. And Roy W. Reaves III, *Archeological Investigations Conducted Along The North Shore Road, St. John, U. S. Virgin Islands* (Florida, National Park Service, Southeast Archaeological Center, Tallahassee, 1986).

PUBLISHED SOURCES

Anon., *Reflections Of The Virgin Islands* (New York, Robilith Publications, nd).

Betsy Bradley and Elizabeth Rezende, *Captured in Time: 1919* (Virgin Islands, Island Perspectives, 1987).

Devereux Butcher, *Exploring Our National Parks and Monuments* (Washington, D. C., Judd and Detweiler, Inc., 1960).

Frederik C. Gjessing and William P. Maclean, *Historic Buildings of St. Thomas and St. John* (London, The Macmillian Press Ltd, 1987).

Jeanne Perkins Harman, *The Virgins: Magic Islands* (New York, Appleton-Century-Crofts, Inc., 1961).

Arnold R. Highfield, *Emancipation in the U.S. Virgin Islands, 150 Years of Freedom* (Virgin Islands, The Virgin Islands Emancipation Commission, 1999).

Desmond Holdridge, *Escape To The Tropics* (New York, Harcourt, Brace and Company, 1937).

Ruth Hull Low & Rafael Valls, *St. John Backtime, Eyewitness Accounts from 1718 to 1956* (St. John, U.S. Virgin Islands, Eden Hill Press, 1985).

David W. Knight, *A Brief History of the Cinnamon Bay Estate on St. John in the Danish West Indies, 1718 - 1917* (St. Thomas, USVI, Little Nordside Press, 1999).

Ruth Moolenaar, *Profiles Of Outstanding Virgin Islanders* (Virgin Islands, Department of Education, 1992).

Karen Fog Olwig, *Cultural Adaptation & Resistance on St. John* (Gainesville, University of Florida Press, 1985).

Karen Fog Olwig, *The Land is the Heritage* (Denmark, Division of Social Sciences University of Copenhagen, 1994).

Alan H. Robinson, *Virgin Islands National Park, The Story Behind The Scenery* (Las Vegas, Nevada, KC Publications, 1974).

Index

Index

Index

Index

Notes

Other works relating to the history of the Virgin Islands published by

Little Nordside Press

A Brief History of the Cinnamon Bay Estate on St. John in the Danish West Indies, 1718 - 1917
David W. Knight (St. Thomas, USVI, Little Nordside Press, 1999), ISBN: 1-891610-05-8.

Into the Light; The Enigmatic History of Water Island in the Danish West Indies, 1672 - 1917
David W. Knight (St. Thomas, USVI, Little Nordside Press, 2000), ISBN: 1-891610-06-6.

St. Thomas 1803; Crossroads of the Diaspora
David W. Knight & Laurette de T. Prime (Editors); Gary T. Horlacher (Translator) (St. Thomas, Little Nordside Press, 1999), ISBN: 1-891610-03-1.

The 1688 Census Of The Danish West Indies [Portrait of a Colony in Crisis]
David W. Knight (Editor) Gary T. Horlacher (Translator) (St. Thomas, Little Nordside Press, 1998), ISBN: 1-891610-01-5.

Virgin Island Exodus [The United States Citizen's Identification Card System of 1918 and the Post-Transfer Quest For Opportunity Under the United States Flag]
David W. Knight & Laurette de T. Prime (St. Thomas, Little Nordside Press, 1998), ISBN: 1-891610-02-3.

daypress@viaccess.net